That's What Grandma Says

Written by
Margaret O'Bryan

Pictures by
Adam Heffernan

DIRECTIONS
Must read, Please

In this book, the phrase, "That's what Grandma says", is used often. Please change the "Grandma" to your familiar grandma name. Such as, "That's what Nana says", or "That's what Granny says". This will make it a more personal story for your grandchild.

We know that self esteem is built by our belief systems. It is true that we can become what we believe. Positive or negative beliefs can influence our lives. You know that children love repetition, so please read this book often and have your grandchild repeat the loving, positive affirmations, indicated by the symbols below.

My Grandma's Name is:

_____ _____ _____
first   maiden   married

Grandma was born on _____.
In: _____. M/D/Yr

I was born on _____,
In: _____.

My name is: _____,

**and I am the most beautiful
child in the whole, wide world.**

That's what Grandma says.

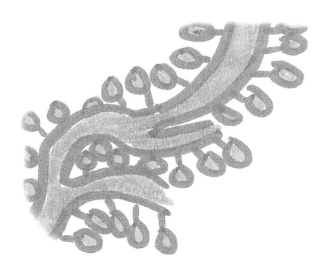

I am special because I belong to God's family and to my human family.

There is no other child exactly like me in the whole, wide world. There never has been and never will be another me.

I am unique.

That's what Grandma says.

I am sparkly because God lives in me.

I am like the shiny stars on a dark night.

Each star lights up the sky around it and I light up everyone around me.

I am so very bright and sparkly.

That's what Grandma says.

I am wonderful because I am full of wonder. Elephants amaze me and so do ants.

I share my excitement with everyone.

I am pure delight.

That's what Grandma says.

I am curious because I want to learn.

I ask many questions. Sometimes, I am not happy with the answers.

When I grow up, I will find my own answers.

That's what Grandma says.

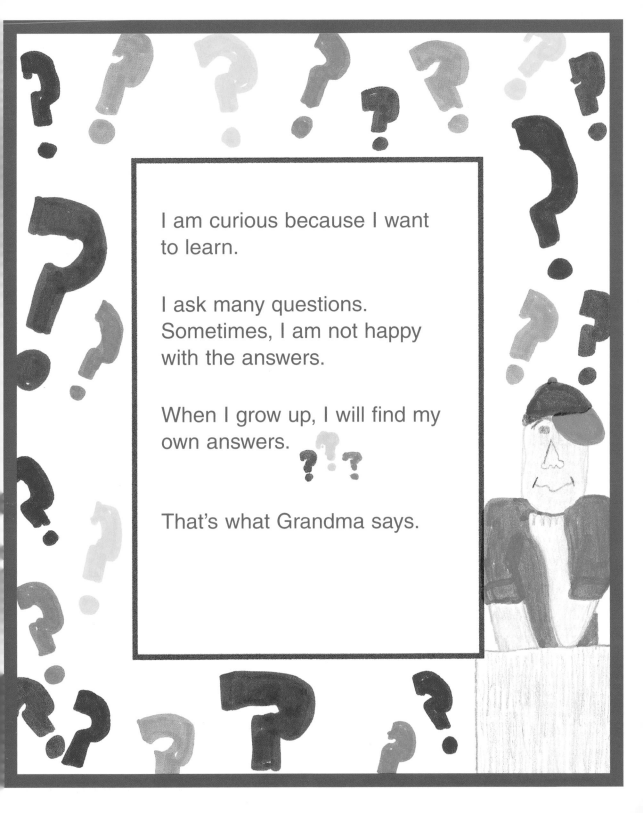

I feel everything because I am
free.

I feel happy. I feel sad.
I feel angry. I feel peaceful.
I feel frightened. I feel safe.

Just like the outside of me
changes, the inside of me
changes too. Because only
God stays the same.

My feelings are always
changing and that's okay.

That's what Grandma says.

I am loved because I am me.

God always loves me no matter what. When I am naughty, the things I do are not liked, but I am always loved.

I am very, very, very loveable.

That's what Grandma says.

I asked Grandma how she knows so much and she said,

"I am still learning, but most of all I am trying to become like a child.

I want to be beautiful, special, sparkly, full of wonder, curious, free and loving.

I want to be like you."

That's what Grandma said.

ME

My Mother

Mother's Father

Mother's mother
&
Mother's Grandma

Mother's Grandma

My Father

Father's Mother   Father's Father

Father's Grandma   Father's Grandpa

Pictures of Grandma and Me

Shared Memories...

_____

_____

_____

_____

_____

_____

_____

_____

_____

_____

_____

... More Memories

DEDICATION

I dedicate this book to God,
who is love,

To grandmothers,
who are loving,

And to grandchildren,
who are lovable.